AF654680

Colour Outside the LINES

By Sarrah Chunawalla

*"Celebrate Differences.
There's no one right way to be human."*

Published By:

Qurate
quratebooks.com
Because everyone has a story to tell

Colour Outside the Lines
Sarrah Chunawalla

Published in 2026
© Published by

Qurate
quratebooks.com

Qurate Books Pvt. Ltd.
Goa 403523, India
www.quratebooks.com
Tel: 1800-210-6527, Email: info@quratebooks.com

ISBN: 978-93-58985-25-2

For Abbas,

and for all those who colour outside the lines

in shades the world often overlooks.

About the Author

My name is Sarrah Chunawalla, a Grade 10 student passionate about understanding people and the stories they carry.

My curiosity about autism began long before this project was even thought of, but it grew into something when I realised how casually people used the word and how a single word can wound along with how much understanding can heal.

I am not an expert. I am a learner.
Through interviews, research and moments of personal reflection, I have tried to understand not just the definition of autism, but the lived emotion behind it.
This book is my small attempt to create a poetic and meaningful space for empathy, sensitivity, and for seeing things through a new perspective. If even one reader decided to "look again", to think before they speak, or to begin their own journey of colouring outside the lines, then this book has done what I hoped it would.

Love and Hope,
Sarrah Chunawalla

Why I wrote this Book

I wrote this book because of a word, one that is often used without thought, yet carries the weight of real lives. For a long time, I heard the word "autistic" being used in ways that felt careless, even cruel. At first I didn't fully understand why it unsettled me. Then I realised it was because behind that word there were people that I loved, and people that the world had misunderstood.

My journey with autism is not academic. It is personal. I have seen how difference can quietly turn into isolation, how behaviour is misread, how silence often replaces understanding. I have also seen patience, resilience, and a kind of innocence that the world does not always protect. Through conversations, interviews and moments of reflection, I began to understand that autism is not something to be simplified or labelled, it is something to be listened to.

This book is not written to explain autism in rigid definitions or statistics alone. It is written to create space for empathy, for pause, and for perspective. It is an invitation to look again at the behaviours we rush to judge, at words we speak without thinking, and at people we do not always try to understand.
I am not writing as an expert. I am writing as a learner. As someone who believes that even small shifts in perspective matter. If this book encourages even one reader to be more patient, more mindful with language, or more willing to meet someone where they are, then it has served its purpose.

This book exists because understanding begins with intention, and because choosing to colour outside the lines sometimes starts with simply seeing people as they are.

Some minds wander,
not because they are lost,
but because they see more.

What Autism really is

Autism or Autism Spectrum Disorder ASD, is a neurodevelopment difference. This means it affects how a person's brain processes information, experiences the world, and responds to their environment. Autism is not an illness, it is not something that needs to be cured. It is simply a different way of being.

Autism exists on a spectrum, which mean no two autistic individuals are the same. While some people may share similar traits, the way their traits appear - and how strong they are felt - can vary widely. Some autistic individuals communicate verbally, while others rely on gestures, visuals or assistive tools. Some enjoy routines, while other struggle when environments become unpredictable. Autism cannot be reduced to a single definition or behaviour.

There are three areas that are commonly experienced differently in autism: communication, sensory processing and social interaction.

Communication differences may involve difficulty understanding spoken language, expressing emotions through words, or interpreting social cues.

Sensory differences can mean that sounds feel louder, lights feel brighter, or textures feel uncomfortable. Social differences do not reflect a lack of interest or care; rather, they reflect a different way of processing social information.

It is equally important to understand what autism is not. Autism is not bad behaviour, a lack of intelligence, or poor parenting. Many autistic individuals feel deeply, even if their emotions are expressed in unfamiliar ways.

What is often labelled as "misbehaviour" is frequently a response to anxiety, overwhelm, or unmet needs. Understanding autism begins when we move away from assumptions and towards listening. Autism is not one story, but many lived experiences each deserving patience, dignity, and understanding.

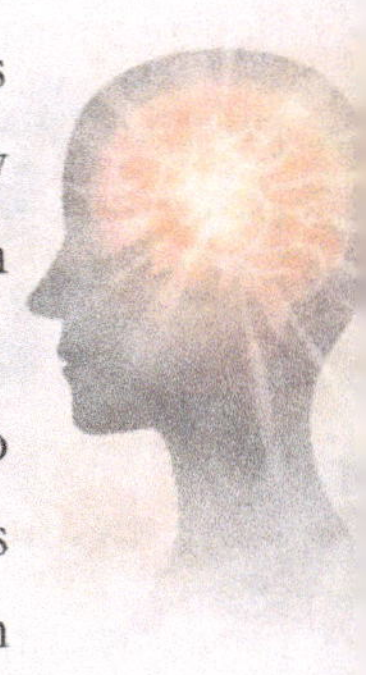

What I learned from real People

Through interviews with a caregiver of a neurodivergent child and the head of a school for autistic children, I learned that autism is shaped as much by environment as it is by neurology. Daily life for autistic individuals is often carefully structured, not by choice, but by necessity.

One of the most confronting realities discussed was bullying and social exclusion. Unstructured spaces such as playgrounds, housing compounds, or social gatherings can be unsafe for autistic children. Differences in communication, body language, or behaviour often make them easy targets. As a result, caregivers are forced to limit access to social spaces not because the child does not belong there, but because the environment lacks understanding. This showed me that exclusion is often subtle, yet deeply damaging.

Both interviews emphasised the importance of structure in creating safety and confidence. Predictability, routine, and guided interaction reduce anxiety and allow autistic children to function with greater ease. Simple changes... calmer classrooms, reduced academic pressure and smaller groups which can significantly improve a child's sense of security.

I also learned that society often expects autistic individuals to adapt, rather than adjusting spaces to include them. Schools, social settings, and even language are designed for neurotypical behaviour, creating constant pressure to "fit in." The problem, as both interviewees made clear, is not autism itself, but environments that refuse to meet children halfway.

These insights shifted my perspective entirely. Inclusion is not about sympathy or charity; it is about designing spaces that allow difference to exist without punishment. When the environment changes, the child does not need to.

Common Misconceptions

Autism is "bad behaviour."

Many people assume this because autistic children may flap, avoid eye contact, repeat words or have emotional outbursts. These actions are often misunderstood as disobedience rather than response to anxiety, sensory overload, or difficulty regulating emotions.

Autistic individuals lack intelligence

This belief comes from the assumption that intelligence is only shown through verbal communication or academic performance. When autistic individuals struggle with speech, conversation or abstract expression, their cognitive strengths are often overlooked.

Autism is caused by poor parenting

Because autistic children may not respond in socially expected ways, families are sometimes blamed, This misconception ignores the neurological nature of autism and places unfair responsibility on caregivers.

Autistic children don't want to socialise assume this because autistic

Many individuals may prefer solitude or struggle to initiate interaction. In reality, many want connection but lack the skills or comfort to express it in typical ways.

Autism is the same for everyone

This assumption exists because people expect a single definition or behaviour pattern. Autism is a spectrum and each individual experiences it differently.

Why Language & Understanding Matter

The pages before this may have felt heavy, or even a little factual. That was intentional.
Understanding must come before interpretation. Before emotion. Before poetry.

Autism is often spoken about without being understood, and language is usually where harm begins. The way we label, joke, or dismiss shapes how people are treated in real life, especially those who already struggle to be heard.

The pages ahead shift in tone. They are quieter, more personal, and more reflective. They are not meant to explain autism, but to invite empathy. To ask you to pause, look again, and consider how words and assumptions carry weight.

Read slowly.
Read openly.

And read knowing that understanding is the first form of inclusion.

To someone who means Well

To someone who means well,

I know you don't mean harm. Most people don't. Most harm doesn't come from cruelty - it comes from words said casually, quickly, or without noticing who might be listening.

You speak with concern. Sometimes even with care. You say things like they'll grow out of it, or they just need more discipline, or at least it's not that bad. You say them as reassurance. And maybe you don't realise how those words stay behind, echoing long after the conversation ends.

What looks like behaviour is often communication. What looks like withdrawal is often overwhelm. What looks like silence is not emptiness - it is processing, protecting, surviving a world that moves too fast and rarely waits. Autism isn't something waiting to be corrected before it deserves understanding, and difference isn't a flaw simply because it arrives in unfamiliar ways.
I don't think you're unkind. I think we are taught to rush. To explain before we listen. To label before we ask. To smooth things over so they make sense to us, even if that comfort costs someone else their dignity.

But empathy isn't about pity, and it isn't about having the perfect words. Sometimes it's about restraint. About knowing when not to comment, not to advise, not to joke. About allowing someone to exist without being measured, compared, or quietly reshaped into something easier to accept. So before you speak, look again. Listen longer. Let difference remain different without demanding explanation or performance. Sometimes meaning well is not enough. Sometimes meaning better begins with learning when not to speak at all.

To Caregivers & Parents

To the ones who stay,

This letter is for those who learn the world twice — once as it is, and once through the eyes of a child who experiences it differently. It is for those who notice things others overlook: the before a pause a response, the shift in breathing, the restlessness that signals overwhelm rather than defiance. You are always watching, always anticipating, always adjusting - often without anyone realising how much effort that takes.

You carry knowledge no one formally teaches. You learn how to translate emotions before they have names, how to guide conversations that don't flow naturally, how to structure moments others take for granted. You teach patience, communication, and regulation intentionally, knowing that these things don't simply appear through observation. And you do it again and again, even when you are tired.

You live with contradictions that are rarely spoken about. You hope your child will be accepted, while also fearing the spaces that may not be safe for them. You want the world to be kinder, yet you adapt to it anyway - choosing quieter rooms, structured environments, and smaller circles, not because your child does not belong, but because the world often forgets to make space.

You are asked to be patient, as though patience is not something you practice every day. You are told to stay strong, even when strength looks like exhaustion, advocacy, and silent resilience. And when you feel overwhelmed, you often carry that quietly, because love does not leave room for rest when protection feels urgent.

This letter is not here to romanticise your journey or minimise its weight. Wanting things to be easier does not make you ungrateful. Feeling tired does not mean you are failing. Holding grief alongside love does not mean you love any less.

You stay. You adapt. You protect. And that staying - that steady, often invisible commitment - is not weakness. It is devotion. It is courage that does not announce itself, but shows up every single day.

Nothing to Prove

You walk into rooms
without armour, without pretence,
without the small ferocity we call ego
—our defence.

You do not make yourself known.
You do not explain.
You do not dilute the pill to make it easier for us to gain.

You simply are.

We, conversely,
carry mirrors everywhere,
checking angles,
softening rough edges, asking to finally be enough in reflections that were never ours to claim.

You do not measure.
You do not compare.
You do not condense joy—
while we stand watching,
unsure what to do with it.

You receive what arrives
and grant it duration—
no translation,
not even the slightest hesitation.
No need to perform.

No need to be legible
to a world that can't wait
for you to become "impeccable."

Where we learn restraint,
you practice clarity.
We stretch ourselves thin,
and yet you remain intact.

Perhaps that's what unsettles us—
not what you lack.

A Word you Throw

When you use the word,
like it's almost weightless,
like it doesn't land anywhere
or hit any spots,

You simply toss it into talk—
use it to mock,
into jokes,
into rooms you don't stay in long enough to see who might flinch.

You don't even hear what follows:
the silence,
the shrinking,
the way another learns
that their name in your world
is just an insult.

That word was never empty.
It carried lives,
effort,
patience-
people learning how to breathe inside worlds that asked them to adjust first

You say it casually.

They live it carefully.

And maybe one day
you'll learn this: language doesn't need intention to harm—
only repetition,
unquestioned,
untaught.

A Letter to my Younger Self

(and to anyone still learning)

Dear me,

I wish I had known earlier that not understanding something doesn't make it okay to comment on it. I wish I had realised that words can hurt even when they're said casually, jokingly, or without intention. Back then, I didn't mean to exclude anyone. I didn't mean to make someone feel smaller. But meaning well was never enough.

I didn't understand how easily silence could become exclusion, or how quickly a label could turn into something careless. I didn't know that noticing someone's difference didn't give me the right to name it, question it, or treat it like something unusual. I thought ignorance was harmless. I now know it isn't.

If I could speak to you now, I would tell you to slow down. To listen more than you speak. To pause before repeating what everyone else is saying just to fit in. I would tell you that sometimes the most respectful thing you can do is nothing at all no comment, no joke, no explanation. Just presence.

You don't need to understand everything to be kind. You don't need to fix people to accept them. You don't need to turn difference into something digestible for yourself or others. You only need to choose care when it would be easier to ignore. There will be moments when guilt shows up. Let it. Not to punish you, but to teach you. Let it make you more aware of how you use language, how you include people, and how easily harm can be done without intention. Learning late is still learning. Growth doesn't lose its value just because it took time.

Some lessons arrive after the damage is already done. What matters is what you do once you know better. Good intentions don't eliminate harm from the picture. That's why meaning better begins with learning when not to speak at all.

With honesty,

Me

Come Closer

If they can be themselves without fear,
why are others taught to disappear?

Some wear difference like a crown,
others learn it pulls them down.

Sameness is treated like a key,
as if belonging needs uniformity.

Quiet is mistaken for a flaw,
honesty seen as something raw.
They are told-softly, kindly—to adjust, to bend, to smooth, to learn the rules of us.

But they are not errors to erase,
not lessons, not a phase.
They stand exactly as they are
in rooms that refuse to meet them halfway.

They are told to rise, to catch the pace,
as if compassion needs a certain shape.

So instead - come closer.
Not to save. Not to correct.
But to see what you chose not to respect.

Sit where laughter fades too soon,
where every silence echoes louder.

Because the wound was never difference—
it was the world deciding
difference did not deserve room.

Why the Misuse of the word AUTISTIC causes real Harm

The casual misuse of the word "autistic" as an insult or joke contributes to real psychological and social harm. Autism is a neurodevelopmental condition, not a descriptor for incompetence, awkwardness, or abnormality. When diagnostic language is used carelessly, it reinforces stigma and misinformation, particularly among young people who may lack accurate exposure to autism.

Research shows that stigmatising language increases social exclusion and negatively impacts self-esteem and mental health in neurodivergent individuals. Even when used without malicious intent, repeated exposure to dismissive or mocking language normalises the idea that autistic traits are undesirable or laughable. This creates unsafe social environments, especially in schools, where autistic children are already at higher risk of bullying.

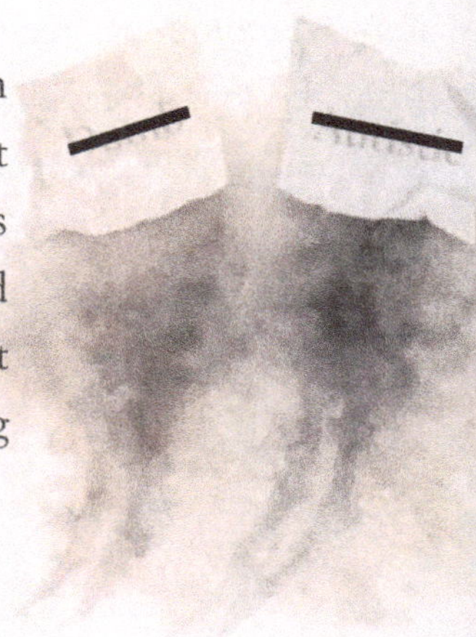

The harm caused by language does not depend on intent. Studies in social psychology demonstrate that repeated derogatory framing shapes societal attitudes over time, influencing how individuals are treated and perceived. Therefore, mindful language is not about being "overly sensitive," but about reducing preventable harm and fostering respect.

How Empathy changes Everything

Empathy plays a central role in shaping inclusive societies, particularly for neurodivergent individuals. Empathy involves recognising another person's experience without judgment, rather than expecting them to conform to neurotypical standards. Language is one of the most powerful tools through which empathy, or lack of it, is expressed.

According to the National Autistic Society, respectful and accurate language helps preserve dignity and reduces social barriers faced by autistic individuals. Conversely, dismissive labels and stereotypes contribute to misunderstanding and exclusion. Language influences how people are treated in classrooms, healthcare settings, and everyday interactions.

Neuroscience and education research also shows that empathetic environments improve emotional regulation and learning outcomes for autistic children. Empathy does not require expertise; it requires patience, willingness to listen, and adaptability. When language reflects respect rather than assumption, it creates space for understanding rather than shame.

What Neurodivergent Individuals wish you Understood

Autistic individuals and caregivers consistently emphasise that behaviour is a form of communication. Actions such as stimming, avoiding eye contact, or withdrawing are often responses to sensory overload, anxiety, or difficulty processing information, rather than intentional defiance.

Another common misconception is that autism presents the same way in everyone. In reality, autism exists on a wide spectrum, with differences in communication styles, sensory processing, and support needs. Many autistic individuals are verbal, intelligent, and emotionally perceptive, yet still require structured environments and explicit social teaching.

Research also highlights that inclusion is most effective when environments adapt to individuals, rather than forcing individuals to adapt constantly. Simple actions, such as clear communication, patience, and acceptance, can significantly improve quality of life. Understanding autism begins when society shifts its focus from "fixing" individuals to creating respectful, supportive spaces.

Where we are
& Where we still need to GO

Parents & Schools : Parents and inclusive schools play a critical role in shaping an autistic child's emotional safety. Schools like Priyanj demonstrate how structured environments, trained educators, and reduced academic pressure allow neurodivergent children to thrive. However, many mainstream schools still lack adequate training, resulting in exclusion rather than accommodation.

Government & Policy: India has taken steps toward inclusion through policies such as the Rights of Persons with Disabilities Act (2016), which recognises autism as a disability. While policy exists, implementation remains inconsistent, especially in mainstream education and teacher training.

NGOs & Community Efforts: NGOs and autism-focused organisations bridge the gap between policy and reality by offering therapy, advocacy, and awareness programs. These organisations often lead change faster than institutions, but access remains unequal across regions.

Acceptance Is Rising, But Not Complete: Awareness is increasing through social media, education, and conversations around neurodiversity. However, casual language, bullying, and misunderstanding still persist. True inclusion requires more than awareness, it requires action, patience, and accountability.

Unsaid

They cried before they knew why,
before hurt learned its name.
something heavy lived inside
them constant, shifting, untamed.

Rooms felt louder than they should,
eyes stayed longer than kind,
and feelings were folded inward,
unnamed, undefined.

When asked what was wrong,
they stayed still.
Not by choice –just never taught how to
feel.

The weight kept growing,
slow and deep,
until it finally broke.
They called it a moment,
a weakness, a joke.

But pain does not need language to prove it is
real.

Some hearts break quietly
long before they are allowed to heal.

A Letter to the Reader

Dear Reader,

If you've made it this far, thank you for staying — not just with the poems or the stories, but with the discomfort that sometimes lives between them.

This book was never written to explain everything to you. It wasn't meant to turn you into an expert, or to offer neat answers that make hard things feel easy. It was written to slow you down. To ask you to notice the words you reach for instinctively, the silences you pass over, and the moments where it feels simpler to laugh, label, or look away than to stay present with difference.

Understanding does not always begin with speaking.Sometimes it begins with learning when not to.

After this, nothing extraordinary is expected of you. No grand gestures. No sudden perfection. Just attention, to language, to behaviour, to the quiet ways harm repeats itself not through cruelty, but through carelessness. To the spaces that ask people to perform in order to belong.

You don't have to get it right immediately. But you do have to choose to be better. And that choice doesn't happen once, at the end of a book. It happens again tomorrow. And again the next time you speak. And again the next time someone different enters the room.

Sometimes meaning well is not enough. Sometimes meaning better begins with learning when not to speak at all.

With hope,
Sarrah

Final Reflection

This project did not begin with answers. It began with noticing.

Noticing how certain words are thrown around lightly. Noticing how some people are asked to adjust constantly, while others are never asked to look again. As I researched autism and listened to lived experiences, I realised how much of what we call "normal" is simply what we are used to, and how easily difference becomes misunderstood.

Through interviews and reflection, I learnt that autism is not loud or obvious in the way people expect. It exists in small, daily moments: in classrooms that overwhelm, in conversations that move too fast, in behaviours that are judged before they are understood. I learnt that behaviour is often communication, and that silence can hold more meaning than words.

Writing this book forced me to slow down. To choose language carefully. To sit with discomfort instead of explaining it away. I learnt that empathy is not about having the right words, but about knowing when to listen, when to pause, and when to stop assuming.

This project changed me quietly. I am more aware now, of my language, my reactions, and the spaces I move through. I understand that inclusion is not a grand gesture, but a series of small choices made every day.

If these pages encourage someone to be a little gentler, a little more patient, or a little less certain of their assumptions, then this project has done what I hoped it would.

Acknowledgements

This book would not exist without the guidance, generosity, and honesty of a few people who shared their time, experiences, and belief in this project.

Thank you to **Ms. Benifer, Head of Priyanj School for Autism**, for offering insight grounded in care, experience, and deep understanding. Your patience, compassion, and clarity helped shape the foundation of this book and reminded me that education, when done with empathy, can change lives.

Thank you to **Farida Vapiwala**, for trusting me with such personal truths. Your openness about love, exhaustion, hope, and resilience gave this project its emotional depth. Your honesty made me understand autism not just as a condition, but as a lived reality shaped by courage and care.

Thank you to **Monica Asrani**, for seeing this project before it fully existed. Your encouragement, feedback, and belief in my writing gave me the confidence to begin and the strength to continue. As a poet and mentor, you helped me find my voice while staying true to it.

Each of you contributed not just to this book, but to the learning behind it.

For that, I am deeply grateful.

Understanding is not an answer.

It's a choice we keep making.

And now it's your choice.

This book is not a guide, and it is not an explanation.It is an invitation, to pause before we label, to listen before we judge, and to sit with discomfort long enough to understand what it is asking of us.

Through poems, letters, and reflection, this book explores autism not as a deficit, but as a different way of moving through the world, one that asks for patience, empathy, and humility rather than correction. It challenges the casual misuse of language, the quiet harm of exclusion, and the belief that difference must always be explained to be respected. This book is for those willing to unlearn, to look more closely, and to choose kindness in how they speak, listen, and see.

You do not need prior knowledge to enter these pages.
Only openness.

9 789358 985252

Printed at Repro India Ltd.